CW00459001

AMAZON KINDLI
GENERATION

A Complete User Guide to Master the
Use and Functions of Your Kindle Fire
HD 10 Tablet, Alexa Skills;
Troubleshooting Hacks, Tricks and Tips

By

Nath Jones

Table of content

INTRODUCTION

Without a doubt, smart phones are a great piece of invention. You can slide them in and out of your pocket and go on to enjoy the multiple functions on the go. Whether you're in a restaurant or stuck in gridlock, or waiting in line to get a ticket; smart phones come in handy to entertain, inform, and keep us connected to the world at any time and any place.

The portability smart phone offer is great, but then there is a limitation: the small screen makes watching videos, playing games and reading e-books a bit stressful. The screen and relatively small display area can make certain activities a little less exciting. This is why tablets like the Fire HD 10 (11th Generation) are just so cool!

If you have used any of the Fire HD tablets in the past, you already know what cool device they are, as well as their capabilities. For newbies, you are about to discover the awesomeness packed in Kindle tablets.

The Fire HD 10 (11 generation) is the new improved model release in 2021. It features upgraded functionalities, improved capacities in both storage and camera abilities, and a host of other upgraded features as you will find out in this user guide.

There are various older models of Amazon tablets but Fire HD 10 stands out because it is faster, and has more sophisticated features. In this book, you will find out all you need to know about this amazing gadget. You will also learn every trick and tip you will need to enjoy this choice possession maximally. And at the end, I promise you, you'll know how to use every single function of the device This promises to be an exhilarating ride, stay with me as we get right into it!

CHAPTER 1

Set up Kindle Fire HD

You may have just unwrapped your first ever Amazon tablet and it is the legendary Fire HD 10, I will show you around this awesome device in just a moment. So, if you are wondering "what next?" Or trying to balance the feeling of excitement and nervousness, I am here to help you set it up the right way.

The first most important and often overlooked part of using a new gadget is getting acquainted with the different parts of it. There are three items in the box:

- Your Fire Tablet
- A power adaptor (May vary slightly in shape, depending on the country you live in)
- A USB-C cable

Below is list of all the parts on your Fire HD 10 tablet:

- An audio jack
- Next to it, is the USB-C port
- Then the microphones
- Next is, the power button, slightly shorter button compared to the one after it
- The volume control button (you can increase or decrease volume with this button)

- Right behind is the rear camera which is a lot better than the previous versions of 3megapixels. It has shot up to 5megapixels
- The front camera for selfies
- There are two speaker ports and the front camera sits in between them
- There is the microSD port. Unlike the other versions, memory space can be expanded to as much as I terabyte, however you need to purchase this microSD separately.

Let's move on to setting up your Fire HD. **To set up your tablet, follow these steps:**

1. Press the power button to turn it on

2. Now unlock by swiping up

3. Select your country and preferred language from the options on the screen

4. After this, click "continue" on the lower right of your screen

5. Connect to your Wi-Fi router from the list of options provided

6. You will be required to enter your Wi-Fi password, after then, click continue

7. Wait for the Fire Tablet to update. It might take a while, depending on your internet speed

8. Once the update is done and installed, you will be required to state whether the device was bought for personal use or for someone else, say a friend or your child. If it is a gift click on "NO"

9. The next page will require to check or uncheck your preferences as regards videos, photos, backups and others. Read carefully through the options and uncheck whichever, however I recommend you keep all those checked and click "continue"

10. Now, it is time for a larger update which you may decide to delay for later if you are in rush. It would take some more time compared to the first but I recommend you proceed with update and get this done with.

11. If you decide to proceed with that, the next page will let you choose whether to make the device kid-friendly if it isn't for adult use. The options are "Yes, create a child

profile" or "Not now". For adult use, select "not now" and then click "continue"

12. The next page will be the social network page which would let you connect your device to Goodreads, Facebook, and Twitter. But if you don't want any of those, go ahead and click "continue"

13. After this, you will be asked whether you want to sign up for Prime Membership. Some pecks of being a member will be listed on the screen but you can decide not to join and click on "No, Thanks"

14. The next page will give non-prime members an option to try a free prime trial and you can still turn it down by clicking on "No, thanks"

15. Now you are ready to install free apps and games. You can select the apps and games you want to install and click "continue" or skip this by clicking on "not now" if you want to install your preferred apps at a later time.

16. On your screen you will get a welcome note just before a tutorial to acquaint you with the features of your new tablet. It begins to roll after you hit "continue"

17. You will see the "home page" and how it displays, click continue and proceed to "content pages" and instructions on how to navigate this will be displayed

18. Continue clicking "continue" through each step of the tutorial

19. The last phase of the tutorial will be on how to use Alexa Hands-free. This feature lets you use your tablet without taking the trouble to scroll.

20. After you have used the trial option, click on "enable" and you can use this option to ask questions and navigate your device easily. (More on this later).

21. Now the setup is complete.

Unregister Kindle Fire HD

What happens if you just changed your mind about the Fire Tablet and want to gift it to someone. Do you have to let them go away with your personal information and all the customized settings you had on your tablet while you used it? No. How about if your device got stolen and you do not want the thief to access your linked social media accounts, emails and other details on your tablet. What would you do? Simple. You only need to deregister your Amazon account and here is how to go about it.

I.   Sign into Amazon.com
II. Click on "Manage Your devices"
III. Select your own device
IV. Click "deregister account"

Note that every app, book, game, and whatever you purchased before deregistering your Fire HD will all be gone by the time you hit that "Deregister" button. So, be sure this is something you really want to do.

Install MicroSD Card

One good thing about the Fire HD Tablet is, it comes in two options which is the 32Gigabytes internal storage space option and the 64 Gigabytes internal storage space option. Although the latter costs a little extra, the both of them can be increased to as much as I terabyte storage space with a microSD card.

Heavy files such as your favorite movies and games can take up a good fraction of the internal storage before you know it. You do not need to go deleting your files to make room for new ones, you just need to purchase a microSD card then insert and install following these steps:

1) Locate SD port on the top righthand side of your Fire HD tablet

2) At top side of the port where there is little tiny hole, open with the edge of your finger nail

3) Insert SD card with the irregular end going inside and the full square edge, outwards

4) You have two options, either to set the SD card as "Extra Internal Storage" or "Portable storage." The first option is great if you are running out of space while the second is recommended if you simply want to transfer a movie or something to the SD card perhaps to watch on another device.

5) Once you select the "Tablet Storage" option, there will be a

prompt on your screen to format
your SD card

6) Next "move content to storage
device" displays on your screen.
if you wish to free up internal
memory space by transferring
content to your SD card right
after installation

7) Click on "Move Content" if you
want to do that immediately or
you could click on "Move Content
Later" if you want

8) If you click on "Move Content",
there will be a display on the
screen showing you the ongoing
process alongside some vital
instructions to ensure the process
is successful

9) Next, you will be prompted that
your storage device is ready to
use. Go ahead and click "done"

10) To see if the SD card has indeed freed the space on internal storage. Slide down the top icons tab and click on settings, then go to "storage" and you would see the details.

Remove SD Card

What if you want to remove the SD card from your Fire HD Tablet? What is the best way to go about it without losing any information stored in it? Let me show you how. Follow this step-by-step guide:

1) Go to settings by swiping down from the top of the home screen

2) In your settings interface, scroll to "device" and select "storage"

3) Scroll all the way down to "safely remove SD card" and click on it

4) Select "Ok" from the dialogue box that displays next

5) Then go ahead and open up the microSD port cap and press the card till it pops half-way out

6) And there it is, you can now remove it.

How to Manage Preferences

We often love to have our devices in a certain way, from what appears on the home page to all the other fine details. The Fire HD 10 is designed to set some of these features automatically but if you do not like what you see, I will show you how to customize these settings and manage preferences. Here is what you should to have your tablet personalized:

> ➤ Swipe down for the top of your Fire HD Tablet
> ➤ Click on "setting"
> ➤ Scroll through each of the items on the list from "display", to "storage", to "accounts", to "security and privacy" options, the other items and set them to how you want them.

CHAPTER 2

Remove Ads and Special Offers

What are special offers? If they are special, they should be some really cool stuff, right? But not quite. They are actually ads you get on your Fire HD

Tablet in exchange for a $15 discount from Amazon as you purchase your tablet. This might seem like a way to save some bucks but after a while, the ads popping up on your screen will become really annoying. Imagine, you are enjoying a nice movie and the ads keep floating back and forth, constituting a nuisance.

In this section, I will show you how to get rid of these Amazon ads. So, let's get right into it.

a) Login to your Amazon account (Provide your email address and password)
b) Click on "Accounts and Lists"
c) Select "Account" from the dropdown
d) Scroll to "Your Devices and Content" and select

e) Click on "Manage Devices"

f) Select your "Fire HD 10 Tablet" from the devices displayed if you have several tablets, you will see more than one but if not, only the Fire HD 10 will be found under "device(s)"

g) Go to "Special Offers" options and click on "Remove Offers" at the lower left

h) Select "End Offers and Pay the Fee"

i) The fee will be the same $15 discount and a little extra for tax. Once payment is made, and deduction is done from your Amazon Account, you will no longer see ads

It is advisable to pay the extra $15 right from the start if you do not like ads and find them annoying. It would save you the trouble.

How to Customize Language and Keyboard

Using the keyboard on your device and enjoying every moment of it would require that you set your auto-correct, predictive spelling, auto-capitalization, and even language preferences. In this section, you will learn how to go about keyboard settings that will make typing easier and hassle-free.

Change keyboard Language

In case you are not a native English speaker or you are using your tablet in another country like an international student studying in Japanese, French or another language, you have the option to set your whole device or just your keyboard into your preferred language. Let me walk you through how to get that done:

To change your keyboard language to your preferred language is pretty easy to do.

- Tap the "search" bar at the top of your screen
- The keyboard immediately displays. Go ahead and hold down the "Space" Bar
- Then various languages listed for you to select from will be displayed
- Click on the search button at the top of this to search for specific language if you do not want to spend some time scrolling all the way to your preferred language

- Once you click on the language
  of your choice, the keyboard
  automatically resets to that
  language

What if the language you want is not
available in the list? Do you know you
could download it? Just follow these
steps:

- Go to "Settings"
- Select "Keyboard"
- Then click on "Change the
  keyboard language".
- Choose "Download New
  Language"
- Follow the on-screen prompts
  and once language is
  downloaded it would be seen in
  the options to choose from when
  you use the steps in 2.2

- You can always switch to whatever language you prefer at any time.

Change Device Language

What if you want all apps and content on your tablet to be in a certain language other than English? Of course, that is possible. Follow this guideline:

- Visit the quick actions panel by swiping down from the top of your Fire Tablet's screen
- Click the "Settings" icon.
- Select "Device"
- Then go on and click on "Change your language"
- Select your preferred language.

Edit Keyboard Sound

You might be one of those who hate keyboard sounds. I do too. It irks me so much that it is the only keyboard reset I do as I do not care much about font styles. So, if you are just like me and you want to mute the keyboard sounds, here is how to go about it:

✓ Tap the search bar on your home screen
✓ Hold down the space bar
✓ A list of languages will display and at the bottom of the list, you will find "Keyboard Settings"
✓ Click on "Keyboard Settings"
✓ Now go ahead and uncheck the "Sound on Keypress" option
✓ You will not hear any sounds again when you type on Fire HD 10

Adjust Screen brightness

The Fire HD is said to be a lot brighter than other Amazon tablets. This function might be great for people who often use their tablets in outdoor settings especially in the daytime. However, if you work with your tablet mostly indoors, you would need to decrease the screen brightness so that your eyes don't suffer from prolonged exposure to the light.

Let me guide you through with a step-by-step procedure to adjust the screen brightness of your Fire HD 10

✓ Swipe down from top of your screen to access the quick action menu
✓ Click on "Settings"
✓ Select "Display"

✓ Tap "Brightness Level"

✓ Use the slider to adjust accordingly

Note that if you leave your "Adaptive Brightness" option checked, your screen will get slightly brighter when you are in a well illuminated place or it will go a little dimmer when you get to dark or dimly lit places. This feature is actually meant to conserve your battery life while also protecting your eyes.

Customize background photo

I am a sucker for cool wallpapers! Yeah. I consider it soothing to have either a photo of a beautiful butterfly perched on a flower or a photo of a clear waterfall with a lush meadow beside it on my tablet's lock screen. If you are also an aesthete and love to have beautiful photos of you or some natural scenery as your background photo, this is how to go about it:

1. Remove all ads. (Follow the steps in the first section of Chapter 2, above)
2. Swipe down from the top of your screen to access the quick action tab
3. Select "setting"
4. Select "Display"
5. Tap "Wallpaper"
6. At the bottom of your screen, you will find different wallpaper options to pick from and also the option, "Pick an image" to select your personal photos from the tablet's gallery.
7. Suppose you do not like any of the photos in the two options in 6,

above. Go ahead and type www.wallalphacoders.com or "wallpapers" into your browser

8. There are loads of wallpapers here but to narrow down your search, enter a keyword, say "flowers"

9. Different floral wallpapers will be displayed and once you scroll through and settle for one, click on the download button i.e., the blue downward arrow

10. Once download is complete, repeat steps 2-5

11. Select "Pick an image"

12. Tap the wallpaper you just downloaded, swerve around the screen to define the points of the picture you want centralized.

13. Then click on "Set"

How to Enable VoiceView

Do you know Fire HD 10 Tablet has a feature known as VoiceView? Here's what the VoiceView feature does. It lets you interact with your tablet in such a way that it gives you audio output. This will be invaluable to a visually impaired person because once VoiceView is enabled, s/he can navigate the tablet with less hassles. In this section, I will show you how to enable VoiceView.

For a brand-new Fire HD 10 tablet, enabling the VoiceView feature is pretty easy. You just need to:

- ✓ Turn on the tablet
- ✓ Select language and location
- ✓ Press the power button thrice and VoiceView is activated to help you with setting up

But if you have already set up and you just want to try out the VoiceView feature, here is a step-by-step guide:

1. Swipe down from the top of your screen
2. Select "setting"
3. Scroll to "System" and click on "Accessibility"
4. Click on "VoiceView" to activate it

Once VoiceView is enabled, there is a long list of gestures you can leverage on to make the experience even more exciting. The good thing is, you can even customize these gestures and have them tailored to your preferences.

Pair Braille Devices

Braille devices enable visually impaired people to read or access information by creating surfaces which helps them translate these pieces of information by touch. It is possible to pair your braille devices with your tablet. To pair a Braille Device with your Fire HD 10 tablet, these are the steps to follow:

i. Enable VoiceView
ii. Swipe down from the top of your screen with two fingers
iii. Tap on "Settings"
iv. Select "Accessibility"
v. Tap "VoiceView Screen Reader"
vi. Tap "Braille"
vii. Select "Pair Bluetooth Braille Display"
viii. Now check to see your braille display is on and visible to your tablet before you hit "Scan"

ix.   There will be a list of braille display gadgets in the list. Find yours and connect

x.   Depending your display type, a pairing code might be requested. See Braille Device documentation for these details.

Customize Home Screen Settings

a) You probably love a home screen that has every icon and app just where you want them. Yeah, most people do. This is why we decided to touch on how to customize the home screen of your Fire HD 10 tablet. Follow these steps:

Go to home screen

b) Scroll through apps and select settings

c) Click on "Apps & Notifications"

d) "Amazon App Settings

e) Tap "Home Screens" settings

f) Uncheck "recommendations" and "show new items on the Homepage"

g) You can go ahead and long press on various apps and move them to where you would like them on your home screen

h) If you still want to go further with customizing your Fired HD 10 tablet, you need to click on "Settings"

i) Tap "Security"

j) And then enable installation of "Apps from unknown sources"

k) Open up your silk browser and type in Apex Launcher

l) Download and install

m) Once installed, your Fire HD 10 tablet will be easy to navigate and customize as your android device

Customize Reading with Blue Shade

If your screen time is high because you are a huge movie, video games, or eBook freak and you want to go on enjoying yourself without damaging your eyesight, this Blue Shade feature is for you and this is how you can customize it to suit your needs:

- Go to "settings"
- Scroll down and tap "Display"
- Then tap "Blue Shade"

- Once you tap "blue shade", you have the option to adjust brightness, color level, and schedule the period (start and end time, days of the week when you want this setting to be automatically effective).

Uninstall Purchased Apps

After several months of purchasing an app, you might realize that you do not quite use it and don't want it to keep occupying space on your Fire HD 10 Tablet. I have good news for you, you can actually go ahead and uninstall them. Here is a step-by-step guide:

1. Select "Apps" from the Kindle Fire Home Home Screen
2. Then tap "Device"

3. Locate the app you want to delete
4. Tap and hold down
5. Select "remove from device"

Or to permanently get rid of dormant apps,

1) Open your browser
2) Copy and paste this link, https://www.amazon.com/gp/mas /your-account/myapps in your browser
3) Locate app you want to delete
4) Go to "Actions" and from the dropdown menu on the right of this app
5) Select "Delete this app" from the "Actions..."
6) Go ahead and remove the app from the Kindle Fire Apps Library Device tab.

7) Note that you cannot delete pre-
installed apps, i.e. apps which
you found on your tablet right
after you set it up

Reinstall Deleted Apps

Although there is no recycle bin on your
Fire HD 10 Tablet, you can still reinstall
deleted apps. Amazing, right? Yeah.
Every installed app from Amazon
Appstore is saved to your personal
amazon cloud library which means that
while it is no longer on your device
maybe because you thought you didn't
need it or mistakenly uninstalled it, you
can go to the cloud and get it from there.

Follow these steps to reinstall deleted
apps:

✓ Go to Home screen

✓ Tap "Apps"

✓ Select "Cloud"

✓ Tap and hold down the app you would love to download

✓ Tap "Install"

How to Force-Close Apps

How do you feel when you are done using an app but it just won't close? Pretty annoying, but there is a way out. It is known as force-closing of apps. Let me show you how to force-close apps when they just won't close:

- Go to "settings"
- Either select "Apps & Notification" or "Apps & Games"
- Select "Manage All Applications"

- Swipe to access "running" apps which would also display the one that need to be force-closed
- Select the app
- Tap on "Stop" and then "OK"

Using the Silk Browser

There's just a lot to catch up with and one way to do this is to browse the internet. You can access the internet on your tablet via your Silk Browser. Using the Silk Browser is very easy but you may need some tips here and there.

Silk is Amazon's browser but it is quite the same with other browsers. You could have multiple tabs running at once, bookmark pages, view browsing history, etc.

To use the silk browser:

- ✓ Swerve through your apps and locate it
- ✓ Tap to launch
- ✓ Enter a URL in the search bar

Just to walk you through the Silk Browser:

You will find about 8 quick links on the browser home page. The first four are bookmarks, history, shopping, news while the last four will be your recently accessed sites

With the page settings option at the lower left of your Silk browser, you could disable the second browser interface on your browser home screen just above the quick links

The silk browser has a right menu (three dots at the top right) and a left menu (three horizontal stokes on the top left)

Tapping the right menu will display some options and at the bottom. There will be a "Get Started" option. You will be asked whether you want to enable "Instant Recommendations." Clicking on it gives permission to your browser to note what sites you visit and recommend similar resources to you

As you play around the menus, you will discover that the Silk Browser is not different from the other browsers on your smartphones.

Pair Bluetooth Speakers

Almost everyone enjoys good music and there's a whole new energy that comes when your favorite song is getting played over some nice speakers. Thankfully there are now these modern miniature speakers which can be slipped into backpacks and moved around with ease. The good news is, you can connect your Fire HD 10 Tablet to Bluetooth speakers and vibe away to your awesome playlist. Let me show you how:

i.   Once your Bluetooth Speakers are discoverable, head over to settings

ii.   Select "wireless"

iii. Then tap "Bluetooth"

iv.   Select "Pair a Bluetooth Device"

v.   Wait for your tablet to scan for nearby Bluetooth devices

vi.   Once you see your speaker in the list, select and wait for it to pair

vii. Swipe down from the top of your screen to see if it has connected in the notifications

viii.   If it has, the next time you need
        to connect the same speakers to
        your tablet it would be much
        easier because your tablet takes
        note of all paired Bluetooth
        devices

ix.   Now go ahead and enjoy a better
        audio experience.

CHAPTER 3

Set Up Parental Controls

Did you just get a Fire HD 10 tablet for your child? That's great but you can also be putting them in harm's way if you let them see everything on the internet. Wondering how to filter out sensitive content from your kid's tablet? Amazon has got you covered with parental control settings. Once this is activated, your child can get to enjoy the tablet without much supervision. Because you will be able to restrict purchases of content, access to camera, restrict video and game access by age.

Let me walk you through the process of setting up parental controls

a) Begin by creating a personal Amazon account. If you already have one, sign in to your account

b) Swipe down from the top your screen to access the quick action panel and tap "settings"

c) Go ahead and select "parental controls" and check the toggle button on the right

d) Tap "Change Password". You will be required to enter a password and confirm password. Go ahead and do that then hit "submit"

e) Now to the more specifics; to restrict content purchases and shopping

f) Sign in to your Amazon account

g) Locate "Account and Lists" at the top right hand and select "Your Account" from the drop-down menu

h) Scroll down to "shopping programs" and click on "Amazon Household"

i) Under "create your household now" select "Add a Child"

j) You will be required to enter your child's first name, their gender, and the date of birth. Provide these details and hit "save"

k) The next page will display your household members including the child you just added and some other details under "Your Amazon Household Benefits", select "Manage Your Content and Devices"

l) You can now enable voice purchasing to prevent unauthorized purchases either using your Alexa App on your smartphone

m) Whichever you choose, tap the menu button and select "Setting"

n) Scroll down to "Voice Purchasing" and click

o) You will be required to add a PIN of four digits after you have toggled on "Purchase by Voice"

p) Once PIN is entered, go ahead and save changes.

Set Up 1-Click Payment

There several payment methods from which you can select when you shop on Amazon but with the 1-Click Payment option, you do not need to enter your credit card details each time you shop online. Sounds great, right? Absolutely! Here is how to set up 1-click payment for your Fire HD 10 tablet:

✓ Login to your Amazon Account
✓ Tap "Account & Lists" at the top

- ✓ Select "Your Account" from the dropdown
- ✓ Click on "Payment Settings"
- ✓ Select which card you want to enable the 1-Click payment for or add a new credit card and click on "continue"
- ✓ Add billing address and hit "continue" to activate 1-click payment method on that card

Set Up Kindle Freetime

Kindle Freetime is an awesome parental control tool every parent needs to have in order to regulate their kid's screen time and filter out content they consider harmful to them from their tablets. Yeah, you want to give your child the best but by all means you must deliberately put

them out of harm's way and this is what
Kindle Freetime is here for.

In case you are wondering how this
even works, here is a step-by-step
guide:

a) From your home screen tap Apps
b) Locate the Freetime App and tap
   on it
c) Click on "get started"
d) Enter parental control password
   and click on "OK"
e) You can add up to 4 child profiles
   just provide the required details,
   name, gender, date of birth and
   set a profile photo
f) Go ahead and navigate each
   child's profile and add different
   content from books to videos to
   games from your own account.

You need to do this to finish up the Freetime set up.

g) After that, tap done and you can now go ahead and create your profile.

Using the Kindle FreeTime App

Using the Kindle FreeTime App is pretty easy but here are some tips as Amazon contributes it quota to making parenting easier in the digital world.

To access your child profiles at any time,

- Tap Apps on your Home screen
- Open the Kindle FreeTime App
- Select "Manage Content & Subscription." Here you can vet what kind of books and videos

are available to your child. If you have more than one child of different ages, you can tailor content according to their ages and that is why they have different profiles

- If you select "Daily Goals & Time Limits", you will be able to set reading goals, screen time (when the tablets should automatically go off (say at their bedtime) and when it should come on in the morning). It can be different for week days and weekends.

- "Manage child profiles" option will let you edit and make changes to your child's profile and see everything from one central point.

- If you select More... you will be able to edit or manage your FreeTime settings.

Add Second Adult to Household

Amazon has what is known as households to keep family members tightly knit in this fast-paced digital world. Amazon households can take up to two adults. some children and teens. Want to add another adult to your Amazon account. Here is how to go about it:

- Sign in to your Amazon account
- Locate "Accounts and Lists" at the top right hand
- Select "Your Account" from the dropdown menu
- Scroll down to shopping program" and click on "Amazon Household"

- Under create "your household now" select "Add an Adult"
- Confirm your country
- Then proceed to enter the name and email address of the adult you'd like to add,
- Agree to share your Amazon Wallet with this Adult, then go ahead and check or uncheck the content you want to share with them and hit continue,
- Go ahead and "Send Invite" after confirming name and email address
- They have 14 days to accept your invite when the invitation email gets to them.
- To accept, they just need to click on the "get started" link in their invitation email

- Then they need to go ahead it continue on the Amazon account and just like you, agree to share their Amazon Wallet with you. check and uncheck what they want to share with you before they can be added to your household.

CHAPTER 4

Amazon fire HD 10 Tablets are great and the user experience is awesome but there is one drawback, Amazon does not allow access to Google Play Store from your tablet. They expect users to turn to the Amazon App Store for Applications but some of the really cool Apps are not (yet) available on Amazon's App Store. Does that mean you will miss out on all of these? Absolutely not! I will take the next few minutes to guide you through installing Google Play Store on your tablet.

Installing Google Play Store

Before we begin the process of installing Google Play Store properly, these are some important points to note:

- Back up all your content and apps

- Remove the microSD card. If you are not sure how this is done, refer to chapter 1

- You are not likely to be able to install all apps such as Netflix even after installation of Google Play Store because Play Store does not recognize your tablet as a Safety-Net Certified device

- There are claims that FreeTime will not be functional for apps from Google Play Store and also, a Google Family link will still not work on Amazon despite installation of Google Play Store

Now let's get right into it:

a) From your home screen, locate settings

b) Tap "Security & Privacy"

c) Activate "Apps from Unknown Sources"

d) A list of apps will be displayed but you can go on and ignore that

e) You need to download 4 APK files; Google Account Manager, Google Services Framework, Google Play Services, and Google Play Store

f) There are different versions of these apps and not just anyone will sync with your device. For your Fire HD 10 (11 Gen) go for Google Manager v7.1.2, Google Services Framework v9-4832352, Google Play Services (64-bit ARM, nodpi, Android 9.0+), and Google Play Store (universal, nodpi)

g) Now let's head on to install the apps, please note that once one app is installed click on "Done" instead of "open"

h) Locate the apps in the "files" app on your tablet and select "downloads" to ensure all 4 apps have been downloaded before you start installing them

i) Installing the apps must follow this order; 1. com.google.gsf.login 2. com.google.android.gsf 3. com.google.android.gms 4. com.android.vending

j) Once installation is completed, hold down the power button and select "restart" from the options.

k) Immediately your tablet boots, scroll through your apps and there it is, your Google Play Store App!

Open the app and follow the on-screen prompts to login to your Google Account. Once done, you can now install different apps from Google Play Store

Quick fix for issues you may encounter after installing Google Play Store:

- ❖ Reboot your tablet: This is very generic but it works. It could just be the way to get them apps running smoothly. Don't underrate it.

- ❖ Google Chrome Browser just won't work: I have come to love Google Chrome; it is in fact my default browser on all my devices. If you are like me, I suppose this is why you were eager to install Google Play Store. So, I understand your disappointment when you turn to it and it isn't working. Here's what to do:

a) Open the Chrome Browser

b) Go to the settings menu

c) Click on "Continue as..." blue button on the screen

❖ What if on trying to open Google Play Store or your other favorite Google apps, it says "this account already exists" what do you do? Simply follow the steps below:

a) Swipe away the app from your recent apps segment

to completely close the app

b) Go to settings and select "Apps & Permissions"

c) Scroll to and select "Manage all Applications"

d) Locate the problematic app, tap and select "Permissions"

e) Turn on all available permissions

f) Then go on and open app again

Or alternatively

a) Go to "settings"

b) Select "Apps & Notifications"

c) Tap "Manage all Applications"

d) Find Play Store in the list of apps and select it

e) Click on "Force Stop"

f) Next click on storage and select "clear Data"

❖ If all of these did not work, then the only way out will be to factory-reset your device. Remember I asked that you to back up your content before we began this process? Now you can restore from that backup just before the installation and have your tablet back to what it used to before you tried to install Google Play Store.

CHAPTER 5

This just might be your favorite part of this User Guide if you love reading just as much as I do. In this chapter, you will learn how to share books with family and friend, download a loaned book, return a loaned book, you will also learn about audio books and how to buy and rent movies. Interesting, right? Absolutely!

Share Books with Family and Friends

Isn't it great to be able to share your favorite books with your family and friends? I feel like there's no better way to create a mental and intellectual connection with the people that matter most, aside from sharing books! So, it is always a delight to recommend books or have books recommended to me by those close to me. If you feel this same way then, let me show you how to do that on your amazon Fire HD 10 tablet.

i.   Login to your Amazon Account

ii.   Go to the "Manage Your Content & Devices" section

iii. Locate Preferences and select "Households and Family Library"

iv.   Tap on "Manage Your Household" now you can select any of the following options: Add Adult/Add a Child/Add a Teen button.

v.   Refer to chapter 3 to see how to complete which ever (household member) category you choose.

vi.   Now select the books you'd like to share with the other adult/child, and give permission to the other adult/child choose which books they'd like to share with you.

vii. Tap "Finish"

Lending new books is a little different and here is how to go about it:

i. Go to your Amazon account and locate the "Manage Your Content and Devices" section

ii. Under Content, click the "Show Family Library" link

iii. Click on the book(s) you'd like to share with a family member,

iv. Tap "Add to Library"

v. Choose the specific family member you want to share with, and then click OK.

Share a Kindle Book from Detail Page

Aside from family members, you may want to share your books with friends and colleagues who have a flare for reading. One easy way to do this is to locate the book's product page in the Kindle Store. Below is an outline of how you can do this:

i.   Go to the Kindle Store on your computer, and search the title you are looking to loan

ii. A resulting list will be displayed, scroll through and click on the book you want

iii. Go ahead and click on Loan this book on the product page.

iv. You'll be redirected to the Loan this book page to enable you type in the recipient's email address and an accompanying message if you like.

v.   Click on Send now to complete the process

Interestingly, you can share books with friends who do not even possess the amazon tablet, they just need to download and install the Kindle App.

Download Loaned Book from a Friend

If you are really a bookworm, you will agree that your monthly book budget cannot get you all the amazing titles you are dying to read. You are not alone. But there is a way out with your Fire HD tablet in your hand, you can request your friend to loan you a book.

Although it is important to note the following:

- Not all Kindle books are available to be loaned
- You have only 7 days to download the loaned book before it is returned to your friend's library
- From the time of downloading your loaned book to 14 days, you have to return the loaned book
- Your friend has no access to the loaned book while it is with you
- Any given book can only be loaned once

So, let's go into how to download a loan book and dive right into it before the loan period expires. Once you receive an email notification with the subject line "A Loaned Book for You", here's what to do:

- Open the email message
- Tap the "Get your loaned book now" button and the link will open in your web browser.
- Provide email address and password and Sign in to your Amazon account
- Specify the device you want to have the book delivered to. Might be your Fire tablet, Kindle e-book reader, or the Kindle app,
- Then go ahead and tap on "Accept loaned book"

Return a Loaned Kindle Book

Suppose you finish reading the loaned book before the 14-day loan period expires, can you go ahead and return it? Absolutely. Especially if you know your friend is eager to have it back perhaps for a class group work or for whatever reason. This is step-by-step guide on how to return a loaned kindle book:

- Provide login details and log in to your Amazon Account
- Locate the "Manage Your Content and Devices" page.
- Tap on the "Actions" button right beside the book you want to return
- Choose "Delete" from the dropdown options.
- Confirm the return by clicking on "Yes"

Download Books to Kindle Fire

Whether you are getting books from Amazon stores or third-party sites you will want to have them downloaded to your device for easy accessibility. Let me walk you through the process of doing both.

For books you have Purchased before now:

- Go to your tablet's Home screen
- Tap on "Books"
- Select "Cloud"
- Tap the book you wish to download.
- It will automatically become available in the "Device" section

For new books

- From Home screen,
- select "Books".
- Tap "Store".
- Enter the title of a book to search for the book.

- Make your choice, then select "Buy"

- Sometimes, there is an option to "Try a Sample" for most books. However, Prime members could have an option to "Borrow for Free"

Transfer Books to another Device

Sometimes you might need to transfer books from your Fire HD 10 tablet into another device, say your PC or a cellphone. Perhaps the books are already taking up so much space or you just want to have them on those alternative devices so that when one battery is flat you can continue reading before you are home to recharge your battery. This is how to transfer books to another device:

- Login into your Amazon account
- Click on "Account & Lists"
- Scroll down and select "your content and devices" from the Menu
- All the books will be displayed
- Select the books you want to move by checking the box on the Lefthand side of each book
- Click on "Deliver" at the top of the screen
- This will open up a list of the selected books and with the Devices' menu where you can select which device to send the selected books to
- You could choose another Kindle tablet, your phone, a computer or

just about any device that you have already linked to your Fire HD 10 Tablet

- Then go ahead and click on "Deliver"

Alternatively

Remember that all your books are stored in Amazon cloud and once you sign into your Amazon account and access the cloud storage on any device, you can have those books downloaded to that particular device.

Buy and Manage Newsstand Items

Do you enjoy periodicals such as dailies, quarterly digests, fashion magazines, etc.? Then you need to take some time to explore Newsstand considering the rich color display of Fire HD tablets, I can guarantee that you will enjoy every moment of browsing through those color magazines. It will only take a few minutes to find your way, let me guide you:

- Go to the Homepage of your Fire HD Tablet and tap on "Newsstand"
- Then click on the "Store" button and several categories will be displayed
- Some Featured Magazines give a 30-day free trial and those are first displayed at the top. Swiping left or right will help you scroll through them and see an offer that might interest you.
- Right beneath these free trials, there are various categories

displayed. They include Bestsellers, Entertaining, Business & Investing, and so on. Note that the order of the list is not constant, however you can click on "See All" above all categories and see the full catalogue.

- Once you make up your mind about which item you want, tap on it

- You will now see the price, a brief description of that publication and an option to either subscribe or buy a particular issue of the magazine

- Once you tap on either of these options, a download action begins but if you decide on it while the download is ongoing, you can click on "cancel" otherwise, when download is complete tap on "Read Now"

- Bear in mind that the magazine you just subscribed to or just bought an issue of, has been downloaded to your Amazon Cloud and can be downloaded to your device at a later time.

Purchase and Listen to Audio Books

I think audio books are great. I mean you can be busy doing the dishes and making dinner without missing out or keeping that novel on hold because your hands are busy dicing vegetables and you need your eyes on it. The Fire HD 10 Tablet has a really nice pair of speakers but you can also connect a

Bluetooth speaker to it to make it even louder.

Want to purchase and listen to audio books on your tablet? Follow these steps:

- From your Home Screen locate and tap the "Audible App"
- Tap the shopping cart in the top right corner of AudioBooks Store Homepage
- You have the option to either search for a book or use the menu on the left to find the book of your choice by genre
- You could purchase a book with your credit card or with the credits you have as an audible member.
- If you are not audible member, go ahead and click on "get this for

Free" and the 30-day free trial audible membership will become activated.

Buy, Rent & Download movies

Perhaps you want to catch up with some movie series you have come to deeply love, or some new movie your friends won't stop talking about, the Fire HD Tablet will let you enjoy movies whether through purchasing them, renting or downloading the movies.

In this section, I will give you a step-by-step guide on how to buy, rent & download movies on your tablet:

I.   Tap Videos from your Home screen

II.   The Videos content library will automatically display

III. Go ahead and use the search button

IV. Type in the title of the movie or a keyword

V. A list of suggestions will be displayed

VI. But go on and hit the search sign at the lower right of your keyboard

VII. Search results will appear. Scroll down and once you find the exact movie you want, tap the title.

VIII. The product page for that title will be displayed to enable you read movie details or even watch a trailer

IX. Once satisfied, you now have to decide whether to Rent or Buy the movie.

X. Whichever you choose, you will have to pay some money.

However, it is cheaper to rent a movie than to buy a movie.

XI. As soon as your purchase is processed, and you then have twos options, to watch now or download the movie to your Fire tablet.

XII. If you rented the movie you have to choose any 48hours within the next 30 days to start and finish watching it. For a rented movie, you can watch immediately by clicking "watch now" or download to your tablet and obey the "48 hours in 30 days" rule else it will automatically become unavailable after that period.

XIII. If you bought the movie, you have it for the keeps.

XIV. In either case, if you choose to download and watch later,

Amazon alerts you how much Gigabytes you will spend per hour of download, depending on the quality you want. The options are 'Best', 'Better', 'Good', and 'Data Saver'. If you like your movies with sharp, sleek images, you do know which to go for!

XV. Please note that downloading series movies have to be done per episode. However, you can add multiple episodes and have them download in a queue.

Turn on Subtitles

Some of your favorite movies and shows might be in foreign languages which you do not understand. Will you have to miss out on all of that? Absolutely not. Your Fire HD 10 allows for turning on subtitles and amazingly it is super easy to do. Let me guide you through it:

- Swipe down to access the quick actions menu
- Tap "accessibility"
- Go on and turn on the toggle button next to "Subtitling"
- To decide how you want subtitle text color, size and background to be, go to "Subtitling Preferences" to adjust these fine details to your taste
- Please note that ssubtitling can only be enabled for supported TV shows, and movies in Prime Video, and also for videos available within the Amazon Silk Browser

- Also, while browsing Prime Video movies and TV shows, the CC symbol on overview page, indicates that any given movie includes subtitles. Although subtitles are mostly in English, other languages may be available.

Purchase Book as a Gift

Gifting books can be so elating. It feels like making actual contributions to your friend's mental growth! With your Fire HD Tablet, you do not only get to read books across genres, you can actually gift books to your nerdy friends.

In this section, I will show you how to go about it;

I. Visit the Amazon eBooks section via this link

II. Search by typing in title if you already have a book in mind or simply scroll through and pick any random book of your choice

III. Once you click on the book you want to gift you will read a short description, listen to an audible sample, read reviews and other details

IV. Scroll down to "buy for others" you could gift this book to an individual or purchase it for a group in case you belong to a book club

V. Specify the number of copies you want to gift where it says "quantity" and hit "continue"

VI. Enter the recipient's email address, type in your name as the sender and also an accompanying message if you wish.

VII. Hit "Verify and Pay Now". Soon after payment is made, you will get a confirmation email and your recipient will also be notified via email about your gift and how they can redeem it.

VIII. To distribute a book gift among multiple recipients, there are two ways to go about it after you select the quantity and make payment. one of them is to send emails with redemption links individually, or use a special email template then fill it with the name of each recipient and redemption links.

IX. Note that you can request refund for unredeemed gifts and you need to be resident in the same country as your recipient(s).

Redeem Book as a Gift

For book lovers, getting a book gift is just as heart-warming as receiving flowers from one's partner. Believe me, that's no exaggeration! Here's how to redeem a book gift on your tablet:

I.   Once you receive the notification by email, tap on "Redeem your Gift"

II. Go ahead and select "Redeem Now" and provide login details for your Amazon account

III. Select the Amazon device you want your gift delivered to. Might be your tablet or the Kindle App

IV. Note that you cannot redeem book gifts from friends who are not resident in your country and the gifts might be returned except there is an option for you to get a gift card equivalent for the book.

CHAPTER 6

Download and Install Apps

There are several ways you can download and install apps on your fire HD 10 Tablet. In this section, I will give you the details for every option and you can go ahead and choose the most convenient.

A. From Amazon App Store

1. Swipe left on your home screen and tap on the AppStore application

2. Scroll through the app to locate the app you want or simply use the search option

3. Hit the "Get App" option and then the "Download" button after

4. The app will be downloaded and installed on your device

B. Google Play Store

This is an option if you followed through with our installation guide for Google Play Store App in Chapter 4.

1. Locate the Google Play Store App
2. Tap on it and search for the app of your choice
3. Click on "Install" and the app is downloaded and installed on your device.
4. Note that not all Google Apps are compatible with your Amazon tablet.

C. Push Up from Amazon Website

To install apps from Amazon Website, push up, do this:

1. Open up your Silk Browser,
2. copy this link https://amzn.to/1H7ClGl and paste it the search bar to access amazon Appstore
3. Navigate to the app you want to download
4. From the app page, choose your device in the "Deliver to" drop-down menu,
5. Then select "Get Ap''

D. Third-Party Sites

You can actually download and install APK files from third-party sites too although Amazon doesn't quite recommend it. Here is how to go about it:

1. Go to "Settings"
2. Select "Security"

3. Click on "Apps from Unknown Sources" and switch it "On".
4. With your Silk Browser, visit the website you want to download from or go to APKMirror
5. Download the APK file from the website.
6. Swipe down to see the notification area at the top bar. It would show download progress. Tap it as soon as the download is completed.
7. Select "Install"

Download and Install Games

One of the pecks of having a Fire HD Tablet over a smartphone is the 10+ inch display area which is great and enhances the thrill of playing games.

With your tablet you can download and install some of your favorite games and simply game away.

Let me show you how:

1. To see the collection of games available for downloads, swipe to Games & Apps or simple click on the Games app
2. Select a game from your Library to download it or search for a new game in the Store.

Zoom App

Many businesses and schools have turned to Zoom for meetings, and classes because of the pandemic. During the lockdown for instance, it was such a great way to keep in touch when simple gestures like hugs and handshakes became death traps. The popularity of Zoom is not going away soon, hence I want to show you how to install the Zoom App on your Fire HD 10 Tablet and catch up with friends or join any corporate meeting.

Although you can join a Zoom meeting without having to create an account but you cannot host a Zoom Meeting or even keep track of your business meetings without an account. Let me show you how to do it:

I. Locate the Amazon AppStore on the Home screen

II. Search for Zoom in the Appstore

III. Tap on it and select "Get App"

IV. It will automatically get downloaded and installed on your tablet.

V. Open the app with a tap

VI. Click on "Sign Up" on the welcome page. There are other options such as "Sign In" (for previous account owners) and the "Join a Meeting" option if you just received an invitation to join a meeting

VII. Type in the email address that you want to use for your zoom account, then enter your first and last name.

VIII. Tap on the box next to "I agree" to the Terms of Service."

IX. In the top-right corner, click "Sign Up"

X. A confirmation email will then be sent to the email address you entered.

XI. Open your email app and check your inbox to see a message requiring you to activate your zoom.

XII. Go ahead and click "Activate Account" or paste the link provided in your browser

XIII. Now set a password and confirm the password by retyping it in the field provided. Not that your password has to be 8 characters and contain an alphabet and a number

XIV. Now you can host a meeting or join a meeting by providing details required

Listen to Music and Media

To listen to music on your Fire HD 10 Tablet, follow these steps:

I. Tap "Music" from the Home Screen of your tablet.

II. The Music content library displays on your screen.

III. If you already have some music on your tablet, tap the "on device" option

IV. Or visit Amazon Music Store by tapping on Store

V. Songs that use X-Ray for Music display [+Lyrics] (B).

VI. Tap the Menu button and select album and begin playing music.

VII. Note that the options in the menu button can help you organize your Music content library into playlists.

To navigate the music screen:

I. Tap the backward arrow-like sign to return to previous track.

II. Tap the short vertical pair of lines or the Pause button to temporarily stop the music.

III. Tap the forward arrow-like sign button to skip the current song and proceed to the next track.

IV. Tap the arrows bent into a square once to repeat all the songs in a particular playlist or album. Double-Tap to repeat the current song nonstop.

V. Tap the scissors-like sign or shuffle button to shuffle songs.

VI. Note that if your song includes X-Ray for Music, (i.e. the lyrics appears on-screen as it plays), you will be able to swipe up or down to read through lyrics. Also, it is possible to tap on any line to skip right to that line in the song. Lastly, tap the grey double line several times to toggle between hiding and displaying lyrics.

Play Videos with Alexa

Watching videos on tablets is just about to be a lot of fun for you. Wondering how? Think about reclining on your soft couch and "ordering" your tablet to take you to your favorite Television Show and watching it actually do it without having to tap your screen. Well, that is exactly how playing videos will Alexa works.

Through vocal instructions, you can have your tablet find a movie/TV show and go on to watch it. In this section, I will show you how to use Alexa to play videos:

   I.   Unlock your tablet. Hold down the home screen button until you see a light-blue line and some bubbly animation close to the bottom of your screen.

   II.   Then say "Search for [mention title/name of movie / TV show]."

   III.   Or say "Find [mention title / genre / actor]."

   IV.   Say "Go to (name of channel) channel guide."

   V.   Or say "Play [mention title of movie]."

VI.   Note that to find and play videos in supported apps, say "Play video on *yada yada* app"

You can also stay in charge throughout the whole movie, pausing and replaying or fast-forwarding with these vocal commands:

- Once you find the movie you want, Say "Play" or "Resume."
- If you need to look away from your screen and do not want to miss a scene, say "Stop" or "Pause."
- If you got distracted and missed a scene, say "Rewind" or say "Fast Forward" If you are too eager to see what happens to a character and do not have a lot of time to sit through the movie

- If you are seeing a series and want to go to the next episode, say "Next" or you absolutely enjoyed a movie and don't mind starting again, say "Watch from beginning."
- Say "Search for [mention genre, maybe romance, horror...]"
- To go up and down the list, say "Scroll [right/left]."
- Once you settle for any of the movies on the results list say "Select/Play [mention number on the list]."
- Scrolled to the end of list of want to see more; Say "Show more."

Photos and Camera

It is true that photographs say a

thousand words. One of the pecks of the Fire HD 10 Tablet is that it's got a better pair of cameras. The front-facing Camera for better selfies, Skype, and Zoom sessions and the rear-facing camera can take just as amazing photos and videos. Some of these tips and tricks will come in handy to help you enjoy your tablet's cameras

Take a Picture

- Go to your Home screen, locate the Camera app in the Favourites grid and tap to open the camera.
- There is a camera-shaped sign and a video-shaped sign but they are actually at different points on your tablet depending on the orientation (portrait or landscape orientation)

- If you want to take a still photo tap the camera-shaped sign and it will become bigger
- Once you have your camera focused on the object you want to take a picture of, tap the circular button that's looks like a little camera aperture (Also, the Capture button).
- And there it is, a photograph taken by you in your camera roll.
- To use the front-facing camera, there is a front/rear camera button on the screen to select from.

Take Screenshots

Taking screenshots have come to stay. Make peace with it. Sometimes, it is all the evidence you have that someone said something to you via a chat or email. Of course, we agree that some screenshots can be doctored but it doesn't strike out the fact that it can help you save screens from your favorite website or a recipe card you do not have the time to write out, in just a few seconds. Can I take a screenshot with my Fire HD? Absolutely! And it is pretty easy to do, let me show you how:

I.   To take a screenshot, ensure your tablet is on the app or webpage you want to capture.

II.   Press the volume down button first, but you need to be snappy about it when tapping the power button, to seem as if you pressed both simultaneously. This procedure helps ensure your tablet does not trip off if the "Power" button press somehow registers first.

III. As soon as screenshot is taken, a chime sound is heard and the screen would flash to confirm the capture.

IV. You will see a quick preview displayed, followed by animation pushing the photo to the top of your screen. Swipe down from the top of the display and open notification tray to see a notification that reads "Screenshot captured."

Share Screenshots Taken on Kindle Fire

After screenshots is taken, here is how to share it:

The first method is

I. Open your notification tray and to select the share icon on the bottom of your notification.

II. This will open a basic sharing interface that will allow you to share to user-installed and system applications.

III. You can email your screenshot, share over Facebook or Twitter, print your images using the Amazon Fire's print service, or even share the image with another device via Bluetooth.

IV. Or go to Prime Photos on your device, select the screenshot you just took, then tap the share icon and choose how you want it shared.

CHAPTER 7

Turn on Show Mode

Show Mode is how Amazon compensates you for all the cool stuff you feel like you are missing out on the Amazon Echo just because you cannot afford one. Yeah. With show mode turned on, you can get to see your tablet carry out the instructions you give it through the Alexa App.

Although Alexa responds to questions on weather conditions, time, or confirmation of set alarms with visual information when show mode is not active, with show mode visuals are enhanced and magnified from a distance for maximum visibility.

There are two simple ways to enable Show Mode, I will itemize them below:

I. Ensure Alexa is enabled and say; "Alexa, enter Show Mode"

II. Swipe down on the notification pane at the top of your tablet and toggle it on

Note that as soon as show mode is enabled on your tablet, it automatically wakes up when you walk near it. The display is much bolder and can be seen from a distance.

News, Weather, and Traffic

Not everyone has the time to sit in front of the TV and actually catch up with the news and weather reports. I mean, our lifestyle has become so fast-paced. How would you like the summary of everything going on to be brought to where you are on your tablet? Well, I will show you!

One advantage of owning a Fire HD 10 is the ease of accessing weather reports. In fact, the reports are a visual update and not just an audio weather forecast of a single day or the day after. With your tablet, you'll see a scrollable weather card from which you can get a full week's worth of weather data. Awesome, right? Absolutely!

To enable video-enhanced Alexa news services:

- Swipe up to unlock your tablet
- On the home screen of your Fire tablet, locate and open the Amazon Alexa app
- Tap the menu icon in the top left corner
- Select "Things to Try,"
- Scroll down to the "News" section and tap it.

- Scroll down to the bottom of the screen and select "Discover News Skills" under "Explore More"
- The Amazon Alexa Skills opens featuring Flash Briefing with full video
- Go ahead and watch CNBC, Fox News, CNN, NBC News, or even HuffPost

Set up Email

Managing your email on your fire tablet is easier than you think. But why do I need to set up my email on my Fire HD 10? Well, we live in a world where emails have nearly replaced written letters, handwritten notes and even greeting cards. Aside from formal settings, you also need email address to sign up for many of the apps. Believe me, email accounts are becoming indispensable.

Let me show you how to set up email on your Fire HD 10 tablet:

- Go to Apps
- Locate email app (looks like an envelope with a paper popping out of it)
- Tap on it. You will be required to add an account
- So, go ahead and enter your email address.
- Provide a password and sign in
- You can add more than one email addresses. You just need to swipe right and select "Add account" from the options. Then follow on-screen instructions.

- Once signed in, you will be able to view all emails in your two email addresses without necessarily logging out of either.

Set up Calendar

Aside telling what day, month and year it is, calendars are important to help us keep track of important events such as birthdays, wedding anniversaries and even official deadlines. Using your calendar on your Fire Tablet is super easy only that you might be sent more than one calendar type and here is how to fix that:

- If you want to view only one type or a couple of the calendars.
- Tap the calendar app
- Swipe from the left

- Check the boxes in front of the calendars you'd like to view

Set Alarms

After a long day when you need to get up early, against your body's will, an alarm can be a lifesaver. One or two beeps and you are up in time to beat gridlock and make to the office or school early. Below is a set of guidelines to help you set alarms on your Fire HD Tablet:

- Swipe up to unlock your tablet
- The "Favorites" menu displays at the bottom of your Home Screen.
- Select Clock and the Clock app opens.
- There is an icon at the bottom of the screen, tap it

- The Alarms screen is displayed.

- Go ahead and click on the plus sign (+) to create a new alarm.

- The "Add an Alarm screen" displays.

- Set the alarm time by tapping on the numbers.

- Scroll down and choose an option for repeating the alarm and set alarm tone

- Then tap "Set Alarm"

- The newly set alarm will be on display

- You can toggle on or off the alarm from here.

Set the Time

Setting time appropriately to time zones and understandable formats is very important. In this section, I will provide a step-by-step guide to help you set the time right:

- Make sure you connect your tablet to a Wi-Fi network.
- Swipe down from top of the home screen, select "settings"
- Choose "Device Options"
- Select "Date & time" and set time.
- Ensure the device time at the top of the screen is displaying your local time.
- Go ahead disable "Automatic time zone"
- After 5 seconds, enable the option "Automatic time zone" again
- Check the device time to make sure it displays your local time.

- Note that if this did not work, you will need to restart your tablet and repeat the above steps

Add a Printer to the Fire Tablet

You might be wondering whether it is possible to print from your Fire HD 10 Tablet. Why not? These tablets are printer compatible and can print documents and photos once connected to a printer. But first you need to add your printer (i.e. make it recognizable) to your Fire Tablet and here is how:

- Go to apps from the home screen, tap it.
- The Apps content library is displayed, click on "store"

- Then the Amazon Appstore for Android will appear, tap the search bar at top of screen
- Type in "Print"
- A list will be displayed. Scroll through and tap "Printing from fire hd"
- Tap your printer's plug-in.
- The product page of your printer plug-in will appear.
- Select Free, then tap "Get App"
- Wait for the plug-in to download and install.
- It is likely that you could be asked to agree to an end-user licensing agreement.
- After which your printer has been successfully added to your Fire Tablet.

Print from Fire Tablet

Now it is time to print. Prepare the document or photo you want to print and follow these steps:

Let's say you choose to print a photo from your tablet.

- First of all, make sure that your printer is on and connected to Wi-Fi.
- Select "Print" from the menu for the photo you want to print.
- Scroll through and select your printer from the list of nearby printers displayed.
- Now set the number of copies
- Then tap on "More Options" to select the paper's size, orientation, and set color.
- Now go ahead and hit "Print" and your printer will get to work.

Turn on Game Mode

Enabling Game Mode on your Fire Tablet will let you play games without being distracted by notifications. Why? Because notifications from Alexa or other apps such as email and social networks are suppressed once game mode is turned on. However, game mode is not supported by tablets with child profile.

So, here is how to turn on game mode and game away without any distractions:

- Swipe down from the top of your screen
- Tap on "Settings"
- Select "Apps & Games"
- Choose Game Mode
- Select "On"

CHAPTER 8

Enable Alexa on Kindle Fire

By now, I am sure you already know Alexa, your virtual assistant who helps you navigate your tablet without necessarily touching it. Here is how to enable Alexa on your Kindle Fire:

- Unlock your tablet
- Swipe right of your tablet's home screen,
- Find Alexa in your Apps library
- Download the Amazon Alexa app and it will automatically be installed
- To launch it tap on the Amazon Alexa
- Type in your name and hit "Continue"

- Go ahead and set up phone verification by entering your phone number
- A confirmation code will be sent to you
- Note that you can select "SKIP" and set up phone verification at a later time
- Also, Alexa is disabled by default if you have parental controls enabled on that tablet.

Voice Purchase with Alexa

Voice purchase with Alexa app is such a cool fire tablet feature. It allows you shop on your device with your voice. The device saves your voice and would go ahead and make actual purchases when a buy command comes in your voice. To enable voice purchase with Alexa, do the following:

- Provide login details and login to your Amazon account
- Select "Your Account" from the 'Accounts and Lists' dropdown
- Under 'Shopping programmes and rentals' tap on 'Amazon Household'
- Hit 'Add a child'
- Some details about your child will be requested, enter them
- Click on 'Manage Your Content and Devices' to restrict what purchased content accessible to your child on their device
- You will be requested to add a pin/disable voice purchasing in order to stop unauthorised purchases

- Go on and open the Alexa App on your smartphone and tap the menu icon.
- Select "settings" and scroll down until you find 'Voice Purchasing'
- Now enter a 4-digit PIN and hit "save"

Use Alexa Hands-Free

Alexa Hands-Free comes in handy when you have your hands on some tasks but do not want to go off your tablet. With Alexa Hands-Free, you can go about your chores and still be on your tablet at the same time. Isn't that great? Let me guide you on how to enable it:

- Download the latest over-the-air software

- Swipe down from the top of your tablet's Home Screen.
- Tap the "Settings"
- Tap Alexa,
- Then go ahead and toggle on the switch for Hands-Free Mode.
- For best results when you want to use your tablet from across the room, plug into a power source.

Using Alexa in Show-Mode

Alexa got a lot interesting with show-mode feature. Just like I mentioned earlier, the display is bolder and can be seen from a distance when show-mode is activated on your tablet. Here are some tips you may need:

Once hands-free is enabled, say "Alexa"

Then wait for the activation sound, after which you can ask a question

Interestingly, your Fire tablet can now do everything you think you missed out on in the Amazon Echo Show and Echo Spot. You only need what is known as the Show Mode Charging Dock. Immediately, your tablet is placed on the charging stand of this dock, it switches to voice-operated mode.

With this you can tell your tablet what to do from afar. It takes your voice commands and acts on it, displaying text in larger, and bolder fonts to enable reading at a distance.

Your tablet also suggests actions Alexa can perform while in Show Mode and this makes it even cooler when you are a novice and don't know all the possibilities of the virtual voice assistant.

Using Drop-In and Announcements

Although drop in and Announcements modes are similar to the Echo Show and Echo Spot possibilities. However, Drop In lets you drop into calls with Alexa compatible tablets, while Announcements will allow you make a broadcast to all other Alexa devices in your household. Seems invasive, right? But they are not on by default, you can choose not to activate them.

- Here's a quick guide on how to use Drop In and Announcement modes on Amazon's Fire tablets: Swipe down from the top of your screen
- Select Alexa
- Toggle on Alexa and Hands-Free Mode

- Tap "Communications"
- Toggle   on "Calling" and "Messaging".
- To configure the Drop In feature, set it to "On"
- Select "My Household" and it will allow other devices on the same account to have access to Drop Ins
- You could also extend the option to selected contacts as well.
- Now toggle on "Announcements"
- Say "Alexa, switch to Show Mode"
- Now go ahead and try out an announcement.

Change Alexa Wake Word

The Alexa Hands-Free feature is an awesome addition to fire tablets but suppose you do not want to say "Alexa" each time you want your virtual assistant to get a task done on your tablet, what would you do? First of all the name "Alexa" is referred to as your virtual assistants "Wake Word" and you can change it!

So, when you want to have ask your tablet to play music, set an alarm, make a list of to-do items, stream podcasts, or play audiobooks, you do not necessarily need to say "Alexa, [insert command]." On your Fire Tablet, you can rename your assistant to Amazon by following the steps below:

- Alexa Hands-Free must be enabled first
- Swipe down from the top of your Home Screen
- Tap "Settings"
- Select "Alexa"
- Then choose "Wake Word"
- Tap "to Amazon" to change its name.

Read Kindle Books with Alexa

One of the perks of owning a fire tablet is that it enhances your reading experience by giving you multiple options through which you can enjoy a nice novel or whatever book catches your fancy. In this section, I will show you how to read books with Alexa.

- With Audible audiobooks on your tablet, simply say "Alexa, play the audiobook [insert title]"
- You can then ask Alexa to pause, resume, or stop reading your Kindle book to you with commands such as:
  - ❖ "Alexa, stop reading in 1 hour" when you want to pause for a nap
  - ❖ "Alexa, read louder" if you don't think Alexa is being audible enough
  - ❖ "Alexa, next chapter" when you finish reading the current chapter

CHAPTER 9

Troubleshooting

Not knowing how to troubleshoot any gadget is like babysitting a child you cannot pacify. I know how frustrating that can be, hence I am adding a few quick fix steps to take when your Fire HD 10 Tablet begins to act up.

Problem with startup

Trying to startup your fire HD tablet and it freezes? Do not freak out! Simply hold down the power button for about 40 seconds and ignore the restart option until it shuts down. Then hold down the power button again and wait for it to come on.

Kindle Fire Won't connect to PC

Perhaps you did not connect the right way. Check to see that the small end of a USB cable is connected to the micro-USB port of your tablet and the other end of the USB cable, inserted into your computer's USB port.

Internal Errors

Trying to download apps and you keep getting, an error occurred? Here are some things to do:

Turn your router off and then on again.

Swipe down from the top of the screen and tap "More" > "Applications" > "Installed Applications" > Scroll to the problematic app > Force Stop >OK > Clear Data > OK

Restart your tablet

Reset time (Refer to Chapter 7)

Can't connect to Wi-Fi

Your tablet needs internet connection for optimum functionality. If it can't connect to Wi-Fi, do these:

❖ From the top of your screen, swipe down and tap "Wireless", and then tap Wi-Fi. Next to Wi-Fi, tap Off. After you turn off your Wi-Fi connection, wait for about 30 seconds and tap "On" to turn it on again.

❖ Could be the distance between you and your router. Move closer. From your device, check if you can connect to your Wi-Fi network. If your network doesn't appear in the list, tap Scan from the Wi-Fi menu. If you still don't see your preferred network, you can add it manually to your device.

❖ If you still can't connect to your network, reach out to your Internet service provider for additional help.

Kindle Fire won't charge

When tablet just won't charge do these:

❖ Ensure your power source is on and if that light point is powering other appliances

❖ Check the USB cable to see that it is still in good shape. Also make sure to use the cable along side an Amazon Kindle PowerFast adapter. Else, you might have problems if you are using a cable or adapter that was not designed for your tablet.

❖ Turn off your tablet and plug in,
allow for 15 minutes and turn it
on again

❖ If all of the above fails, get your
receipts and see if you are still
eligible for warranty and reach
out to Amazon Customer Support
either via calls or an email.

Browser not working

If your Silk Browser keeps crashing or
just won't open? Here is what to do:

❖ Restart your device by turning it
off and waiting for 5 minutes
before turning it on again

❖ Go to Silk Browser > browser
menu > browsing history > clear
all

Freezing app

If an app just won't load or keeps freezing, do any one of the following:

❖ Go to Settings > Apps & Games > Manage All Applications > Force stop the freezing app > Clear cache.

❖ You can also restart your tablet, then uninstall the specific app and re-install again

Forgot lock screen PIN

If you forgot your lock screen password or parental controls PIN? Do not panic! You can reset it directly from the lock screen on your device.

However, your device must be connected to the internet to reset your lock screen password or PIN.

a) From the lock screen on your Fire tablet, enter the wrong password or PIN five times.

b) Choose "Reset Your PIN" from the on-screen notification.

c) Enter your "Amazon account password"

d) Then tap "Continue"

e) Enter a new PIN or Password, then tap "Finish"

CONCLUSION

Now that you know all you need to know about this amazing gadget, you can go ahead and enjoy the amazing possibilities of your Fire HD 10 Tablet. Every trick and tip you have learnt will come in handy before you know it. The good thing is you can always refer to this handbook any time you get confused.

Cheers!

Printed in Great Britain
by Amazon